The River of Forgetfulness

The River of Forgetfulness

Poems by Rachel Hadas

David Robert Books

Published by David Robert Books
P.O. Box 541106
Cincinnati, OH 45254-1106

Typeset in Aldine by WordTech Communications LLC,
Cincinnati, OH

ISBN: 1933456248
LCCN: 2006925211

Poetry Editor: Kevin Walzer
Business Editor: Lori Jareo

Visit us on the web at www.davidrobertbooks.com

Acknowledgments

Thanks are due to the editors of the journals in which the following poems have appeared, sometimes in different form or under different titles:

Arion, "Boy Heroes in the Sea," "Three Roads"; *Atlanta Review,* "Modern Greek 101"; *Barrow Street,* "Daylight Saving," "The Wrong Recital"; *Cincinnati Review,* "Bird, Weasel, Fountain," "The White Cat"; *Daedalus,* "Inspissation"; *The Formalist,* "Two Dickensian Moments"; *Good Foot,* "Simile, Analogy, Mimesis"; *Heliotrope,* "The Shadow of Departure"; *Hotel Amerika,* "Dr. Mnemosyne's Office"; *The Hudson Review,* "Boatride," "Lightbulbs and Soap"; *Literary Imagination,* "Pennies," "Tea?"; *Luna,* "Crystal Lake"; *The New Criterion,* "The Nosebleed"; *New England Review,* "The Boulder"; *The New Republic,* "The Progress"; *The Progressive,* "The Gift"; *Poetry,* "Conklin 455," "Triolets in the Argolid"; *Raritan,* "Neolithic Figurine, Spetses Archaeological Museum"; *Saint Ann's Review,* "River's Edge"; *Salamander,* "Blemish," "The Interruptions"; *Slate,* "The Bond," "Impatience"; *Southwest Review,* "At the Goodwill," "I.D. Photo"; *Tiferet,* "Home is the Sailor"; *Yale Review,* "October Cats," "The Verge."

Contents

III.

I.

In My Son's Room, Not Sleeping

Punishment? Banishment? The empty room
already blushes with a hint of dawn.
Blinds pulled down can't stanch the stealthy sun.

If there's a clock in here, it doesn't tick.
Hours pile into a teetering stack
of mornings trumping midnights. Week by week,

haggard from the vigil, time to pay
the tax for restoration of the fray-
ing velvet darkness thinner every day.

Ode to Sleep

O soothest Sleep, if so it please thee, close
In midst of this thine hymn my willing eyes,
wrote Keats. Sleep: the delicious,
the longed-for, the elusive.

To praise and pray for seem redundancies,
close to synonymous, yet opposite:
we praise what we have and pray for what we lack,
but also praise what we know how to cherish
because we have had it but have it no longer
(youth, health, success); and pray for what we wish
continuance of, like happiness, like life.
To assume any good thing
will go on blithely bestowing itself
feels unlucky, so we pray for it.
What prayer and praise both bracket
is blessing. And what else is sleep? It's doubtful
whether Keats managed to close his eyes
amidst the very hymn he was composing
to the moody goddess. He must have known
a cloudy law ordains: who wants to sleep
must put down pen and paper,
notebook and notes, and yield;
drift through the door with hands left floating free
to follow a dark clue.

Side by Side

Are you asleep? Not really.
A mountain pass, a valley
unfurl before your eyes.
Galloping images seethe in your skull.

Am I awake? Not really.
I know where my arms and legs are
and that the cat's head rests against a flank.
I can answer the phone in a flash and sound alert.

But just as in your drowsiness a sly
spark of alertness hides,
so in my readiness to leap from bed
there lurks a dim refusal.

The Interruptions

It's summer, but my window
of concentration's closing.
If no one else will do it,
I interrupt myself.
Yesterday, though the cat
kept threatening to jump
onto the ironing board,
I ironed for half an hour.
More often, though, I walk.
Alone is very good,
but there are people too,
summer friends, fair-weather
and foul, with whom to stroll
sleepy July and August afternoons
and taste each other's troubles
and in an hour or two
return to our separate stories.
When I get home, the window opens wider.
And now a gentle tap.
What's knocking at the door?
I open it a crack:
Plot. Not now. Not yet.
Thank you. I turn my back.

Anton Webern's Dream

in memory of Robert Black

In the early months of my son's life,
still nursing many times a day, I thought
I'd work at home a little
and undertook to tutor a musician
in the art of poetry. His poem
was entitled "Anton Webern's Dream."
I scanned the one typed page he handed me.
Title, epigraph, first line—already
I was baffled. Read the page again.
Read it, reread it, re-reread it: nothing.
Mulishly I asked him more than once
"Tell me, whose dream? Whose letter? Who is speaking?
That quote's from where? Could you explain the syntax
one more time?" But even if my earnest
student answered, and he must have tried to,
something—whether my hormonal haze
or else his way of using language—caused
his replies to skid into oblivion,
unless there were no answers, just intentions.

A decade passed. He died of melanoma
undiagnosed, or diagnosed too late,
treated too late, too lightly—who can say?
There were no explanations, just an end.
At his memorial service
another poet (as it turned out, my

successor as his tutor—I had failed)
praised and then read, though he did not explain it,
the very poem, "Anton Webern's Dream,"
that had so thoroughly defeated me.
Clearly this was his only finished poem,
his only poem. Nothing but the title
had stayed with me—the rest was milky halo,
stubbornly elusive as the dream.

What Color Was His Bathing Suit?

Stories provide materials that frame
a question no one's thought to ask before.
The listener does the asking, but the story
sets up the listener. Once you formulate
your question, is it answered? Yes; but (a)
the answer often asks a further question;
and (b) the story must be put together
in such a way that even if no questions
ensue, it works as story:
beginning, middle, end.

Bird, Weasel, Fountain

Seuss-like with its tufted yellow topknot
and roosting in a histrionic landscape—
snowcapped purple mountains, orange sunset—
the oddly crested bird in one of the paintings
upstairs in the Roerich Museum
stopped me on my last visit. Recognition
passed between us. I remembered it;
it seemed to have been awaiting my return.

Mounted by Balch of Lunenburg, the weasel,
wearing winter white, and with a mouse
eloquently dangling from its jaws,
takes my measure from its pedestal
low in a glass case in an exceptionally
dim corner of the Fairbanks Museum
and says quite plainly, though its mouth is full,
We'll know each other when you come again.

Solemn in their pre-Raphaelite grace;
alert and sympathetic, though reserved;
ready to meet the gaze of anyone
who passes by, the figures in the fountain
at Riverside Park and 116th Street
hold out their shallow goblets, mildly offer
the thirsty wayfarer a drink of water
and silently invite her to return.

The bird is not well painted, and the weasel
is badly lit. The fountain's low relief,
eroded by familiarity,
is hard to see—they all are—
without an effort. All three are too proud
and patient to call *Here I am—remember?*
Given attention, I have things to say
to you, as you to me, if you return.

The Hotel

I fell asleep while reading *Peter Pan*
and dreamed of Tinkerbell
flitting through a vast half-built hotel.
Nubile, slender, fluffy as chenille,
she clambers up onto a balcony;
effortlessly vaults into a room;
lands lightly on the lap of an old man
in a rocking chair by the window. I know him.
He is my neighbor's father, and he died
jumping from the balcony of a hotel.

I fell asleep reading *The Magic Mountain*.
Unless we all inhabit a huge hive,
every town has one such hostelry.
Your carpet's stained? Go on and ring the bell.
Call for a chambermaid with mop and pail.
No, best to travel with a scrubbing brush.
Despite your elbow grease, the lingering spot
will usefully remind you of the name
(matchbook, soap, stationery bear no logo):
The No Good Deed Goes Unpunished Hotel.

Crystal Lake

To live life and to comment on it at the same time—
to meta-live—is the preserve of women,
our province and our presence,
women waist-deep in water,
quietly chatting, not missing a narrative beat.

Look back! What's gaining on you?
A seagull struts over to the towel in search of food
but finds only fishing rods, a book of poems,
a bottle a quarter full of tepid Coke,
and a Santa Fe magazine entitled *THE*

which features an interview with the art critic Dave Hickey.
Everybody knows that your parents are assholes
and your grandparents are really great people.
This is just a given. No more to build on there;
the gull stalks off with its cohorts.

At the far end of the beach,
my son and his best friend and his girlfriend are fishing.
Her narrative is nestling under his;
he will not really speak to me, so neither will she in his presence.
Oh lives of males, untalked-of,

untalking; engaged in the act with no
need to construe it beforehand and no soft
voiceover as it is played out.
Oh symmetries of lake, shore, sky; wide bowl
of—you supply the word. I'm running out of names.

The Dream of the Novel

As long as I read to you,
the world's voice was delivered to you through me.
The world was the book and the book was the world
and I was both. When you had learned to read,
long after there was any literal need,
you liked to be read to
at bedtime, when I liked to read to you.
And when my reading voice became too slow,
you broke the pattern, took the book away
to read yourself. Now skip six years or so.

Last night's dream announces
a new, unsettling chapter opens now.
You have become the book
triply: first that it is yours to read
in the silence that trumps sleep; and next
that the book is about you; and last
that you wrote the book—a novel which,
declares the dream, contains your true opinion
of the world and everything it holds.
Characters! Plot! I can't wait to read it.

You always told me that I read too fast.
Now furtive, hurried, guilty, I leaf through,
skimmingly aware that Mom and Dad
are no longer, if we ever were,
hero and heroine. You are the shaper
of your story; parents figure only
as king and queen whose choice, if any, is
how to pass on their kingdom. But the novel
(I'm riffling through the pages like a spy)
is illegible. Is it in code?

Or am I just distracted, always trying
to do too much at once? Your threefold book
halts at the threshold between night and day.

TPN

In Total Parenteral Nutrition,
glucose and protein
bypass digestion,
detour round the gut,
deliver a direct
hit of strong and sweet.
With TPN, no need
to pick a piece of bread
up in your hand
and lift it toward your head.
Why do the work,
hoist spoon or fork,
chew, swallow, digest,
and all the rest,
when TPN (a phase
learned back in the days
I worked with PWA's)
pumps essences of food
straight into the blood?

And your point is...?
I hear my son's voice say.
It's that my students take
in stories just this way.
Myth bypasses the brain
to sing in every vein.
And yet the savor clings to each old tale.
The tradition's oral;
their mouths are watering, their eyes are bright.

Myth entering them touches where they live,
like TPN,
like drops of mercy's celebrated rain,
needful, delicious, unconstrained and free.

Do you see what I mean?
I ask my son.

Simile, Analogy, Mimesis

Approach this dollhouse world,
a miniature realm
coterminous with and also distinct from
our home place, which it slyly
mirrors. Take one step back.

The pleasure lies in both
the correspondence and the separation;
both in the recognition of likeness
and the exemption from the chore
of actually subsisting.

The tiny dancers, warriors, and gleaners,
flies clustering on a milk pail,
sweaty woodcutters, clamorous flocks of cranes—
we gaze, the mirror glints, and winks,
the analogy drops a curtsy.

When I was young
I never got the point about mimesis.
The notion of imitation seemed at once
inadequate and obvious. I've come
late in the day to the simple satisfaction

of pointing out a thing we recognize
showcased by the dollhouse with three walls.
And something more: mimesis replicates
permanence in a world that is our home
and yet is falling and flowing and falling away.

Courbet Revisited

I crane at a young woman in a shadowy glade,
but my reflected face
obscures her, and my breath
fogs the glass. I take a step
back, then, leaning forward, try again.
A gentleman and a small
tawny poodle docile on its leash
stroll through the loom of worlds on either wall
and pause (one stands, one sits) to contemplate.
Scarlet motes, midges in muggy air
fleck a deer's rump as it bends to drink.

As if the freighted silence were for sale,
someone gestures towards a cold green hill
captured in a frame and asks the price
just a shade too loudly. Whereupon
the poodle and the man each turn their back
on a hilltop chateau half scarved in mist;
a girl with auburn hair spread shining on her pillow;
a pebbly windswept beach
empty but for one abandoned rowboat,
oddly foreshortened, and make for the door.
Lightly the dog's claws clack on the parquet.

The Wrong Recital

The goatherd on his motorcycle never
would have dreamed of trying
to count his long-haired charges as they trotted—
sipping salt water, nibbling orange peel—
along the pebbly beach of southwest Samos.
To number things invites the Evil Eye.
Do not count the pigeons in that flock
wheeling toward the treetops.
Do not count the meals you'll cook and eat,
the students waiting in their seats
as you walk into the room,
the papers they will write and you'll correct.
Whether these seem too many or too few,
they're dwindling. Do not even roughly reckon
the audience in Weill Hall
when Jeong-Hwa Park gave her piano recital.
Of a handful of listeners, I was one.
I was supposed to be at someone else's
concert at Merkin, and my senior moment,
if that is what it was, restored a piece
of what I hadn't realized was lost
so hadn't searched for yet. One remedy
for whatever drains our hours away
is: don't count anything. Another: carry
loss (as in losing; as in getting lost)
deep inside yourself,
close to your heart, where it cannot be found.

The Tag

All last month I kept
throwing things away
until I was exhausted,
scouring out what like
Philemon and Baucis'
hospitable bowl
seemed never truly empty.
But finally there was nothing left in the drawer.
So I went shopping and bought a sweater.

Those plastic tags designed
to raise an alarm if you try
to sneak something out unpaid for—
when I got home I discovered one
lurking near the hem,
as silent as a serpent.
I thought of throwing this sweater too away,
but took it back to be defanged instead.

Memory

Not all two year-olds say No No No
and not all teenagers are rebellious and sullen
and not all older people lose their memories.
So far mine still spells me back the word,
still replaces paragraph or stanza
on the left- or right-hand page of the open book.

Lately this useful servant has shown signs
of turning into a demanding mistress
who stretches her domain to every stance
and chance of sidewalk meetings. Sparrows peck
a frozen bagel. One white shoe a strollered
toddler has presumably kicked off
has been rescued by a passerby,
laid on the stoop for someone else to find.

Not that the ruthless mirror isn't pocked,
cloudy, flawed. But gaps are papered over
with guesses, phrases, scraps of poetry.

The Progress

Soft missiles hitting home release a shaft
of call it light from nowhere (what they touch
has waited a long time
for this illumination); then drift off
transparently, with no more fuss than sunlight
when it crosses a lawn from dawn to dusk.
How effortless and easy? Don't believe it.
How fugitive. Recall
with what birdlike brushings Memory
revisits—not at our behest, but when-
ever it pleases her to pass our way,
with a regard now open to the sky,
now narrow as a cat's
eye in the afternoon. A single slit
accommodates all span, growth, change; a single
golden dust-mote-studded ray picks out
a pair of hands
swabbing a counter, smoothing a child's hair,
taking something silken from a box,
holding it up, shaking it out to air.

Delete, Expunge

Afternoon spent doggedly deleting emails.
Are my spots finally changing after thirty years
to match my quiet husband's? Am I treading
in the footsteps of Carolyn Heilbrun,
who in her last years divested herself
of the social swaddling most women
spend our lives involved in? Or is this
nausea nothing more than the hangover
following too much talk? Time does its work
deftly, with a minimum of chitchat;
I pledge to do the same, only to find
I'm picking at the selvages of silence.

The sunlit colors of a dawn dream do
manage to translate—barely—into words,
but are not words. They come from deep inside
my skull and surface mute
until with clumsy paws I set them down
and free as language, whereupon
I turn to press the keys: DELETE; EXPUNGE.

A Broad Margin

The mind well-stocked and empty, both at once,
dumbly waiting for something to appear
on the horizon while at the same time
flipping pages which are both pristine
with possibility and grubby grey
with annotation. Thoreau wrote: *I love*
a broad margin to my life. Most likely
he jotted these eight words down in some margin,
protective hedge between the little volume
held in his hand and the heavy tome of the world.

At the Goodwill

Not right away, but after a good while
in a patient line at the Goodwill,
I spied a woman in a wheelchair wedged
into a corner behind the counter. Two
women manning the cash register
blocked a clear view of her:
she wasn't difficult to overlook.
But once I saw her, I felt free to stare
(and had the time—the line moved at a crawl).
Thick gold-brown hair
fell over her face. She was untangling
a necklace of gold strands with busy hands,
and pausing sometimes to report
on her progress to her colleagues there.
Once she looked up.
 Huge asymmetrical
blue eyes: I couldn't tell
her age, or even whether she was blind.
She had a kind
of beauty, and it rang a distant bell.

I, who can barely think from A to B,
do math, decode a map, or find my way,
cannot not remember what I read.
Yes! She reminded me
of the Dolls' Dressmaker in *Our Mutual Friend*,
Miss Jenny Wren:
the golden hair, the high

hunched shoulders, busy fingers, young-old face,
child-woman cramped from morning until night
doing delicate needlework ("I can't
get up," she tells her visitors, "because
my back is bad and my legs are queer"),
boxed into an obscure
sweatshop whether in a London garret
or Swarthmore mini-mall
where we stood in line at the Goodwill
waiting to purchase an immense recliner
for my son's room this fall.

Two Dickensian Moments on Morning Talk Shows

Preserving Your Wedding Gown

Since I am waist-deep in the past,
this expert on TV,
peculiar though her subject is,
has much to say to me.

Memories I understand.
Photographs? Fine, okay.
Sentiment, reverence for the past,
and continuity?

Certainly. But this new field,
Wedding Gown Preservation—
how to keep that gown pristine
for the next generation—

takes the whole memory business,
in my students' phrase,
to another level.
In treated paper, swathe

the specially treated dress and veil.
Arrange them, dormant loves,
folded in a special box.
Put on special gloves

to unfold and admire; touch
with a cotton fingertip.
Don't hold the folds against a cheek
or brush them with a lip.

Once you have checked that they're intact,
shut up the box again.
These are fragile fabrics.
Just ask Miss Havisham.

Take Care of Him, He Bites

Program on child psychology, ominously titled
Children Who Bite. Onscreen: a knot of kids
facing away from the camera;
one girl's auburn hair seen flowing down her back.
They're closely clustered in a schoolyard, gazing
at somebody whose presence can be felt
from the pressure of eyes we viewers cannot see.

Having bitten Mr. Murdstone's hand,
David is packed off to Salem House.
It's still vacation; he's at school alone.
A wooden sign awaits him in the classroom.
He has to hang the specially painted thing
around his neck and wear it all day long,
first in the empty corridors, and then
in the schoolyard, when,
holiday over, his schoolmates
avidly return.

Inspissation

Definitions. Density. Conundrum.
Condensation. Etymology.
Abstraction and the hissing as of air
escaping. And indeed, the atmosphere
becomes so thick that vision fogs
up like a windshield in the wet.
Socked in: was this what the word meant?
The bright and baggy globe gone blank,
the world, capacious, starts to shrink:
tugging of tendrils, tightening
of texture, so our habitat,
already a snug fit, begins
to fold its wings, draw in and in.
Crisscross of kinships, instances,
recognitions and reunions,
coincidences, fertilizations
at an ever thickening pace,
blanket of fog and muffling mist,
crosshatching of the busy thin
but countless filaments scribbling
to chiaroscuro, then obscure,
almost opaque, unnumbered, slight
only if taken one by one,
but thickly strewn, oh I am caught,
the small world tighter, smaller, clasps me,
blinds me: inspissation.

Marginalia

When books were precious, in the Golden Age,
students were taught not to mark up a page.
Later: *Read with a pencil in your hand.*
Taking notes will help you understand.
Still later, highlighting became the fashion:
color the text and never mind the margin.
In this way each correction, annotation,
tart contradiction, literal translation,
all marginalia, safe from the limelight,
managed to go on hiding in plain sight
in an abundance that no one suspects
for whom to read means flipping through a text.
Who scans and skips misses the ghostly power
of all the readers who have come before.
Margins, with boundless, unobtrusive patience,
outlast one life by many generations
and form a zone where one can all but touch
the minds of readers decades out of reach.
Potentially, the measliest annotation
helps us determine by triangulation
what some previous peruser thought
when they felt impelled to make a note.
What bell rung by Lucretius in Book Four
made my father jot the name "Pasteur"
in pale blue pencil? Easier to see
why in *Henry V* (scene ii, Act III)
my brother wrote "Huck Finn," reminded by
the conscience-stricken Boy's soliloquy.

Examples are unlimited. To read
isn't charging blindly on ahead.
You hold what someone wrote—it's called a book.
But someone earlier may have left a track
which if you pay attention leads you inward, backward toward another person's brain.
Intimate privacy: reader as sleuth
on the winding trail of call it truth.

In *Pnin,* the eponymous hero gets to see
in a collection of French poetry
he's borrowed from the college library
some student's annotated carefully
"in purple ink the difficult word *oiseau*"—
the gloss above, the foreign word below,
while nested in between them broods a bird,
wings softly folded, hatching out the word.

II.

October Cats

One is the color of graham crackers and milk;
cornbread with butter and honey;
a stack of pancakes drenched with maple syrup;
peaches and cream (is anybody hungry?).
The other's tiger markings, grey and white,
are lit like alabaster from within,
foxy, rosy, ruddy; dusky blush.
Who would have thought we were so famished for
the tawny, the caressable? No longer
now splayed out along the floor for coolness,
they reconfigure for the coming season
into shapes of meatloaf, tugboat, owl.

Pennies

Almost daily now I seem to stoop
to the icy sidewalk to pick up
pennies in my path—each one a crumb
scattered along a gloomy forest trail
toward either safety or the witch's cottage.
If I ignore them, who will pay attention?
Pocketing them, do I know where they lead?

About the time you start to think of death
more often than occasionally is when
the story's end, the closed parenthesis
slides into view in silence. Yes, the foreground
teems: reunions, holidays, and shrieks.
But look up, look above the revellers' heads
at the horizon, at the deepening light.

Twenty-two, Married, on a Samian beach

The world was to be walking side by side
and hand in hand and sleeping curved as spoons
and raking sea-wet pebbles
with twenty toes and gazing
at the sun slipping into the Aegean
and the afterglow. Contrast the wrench
and aftershock of stoppage: fast, then slow.

Since *world* meant *future*,
world enough and time
meant one thing and the same:
seconds to set down and years to live through.

The Boulder

This black boulder at a bend in the Water
Andric, almost massive enough to be a
meteorite, cannot have really shifted.
   Still, something's different.

Has the curve of road or of brook changed? I can't
seem from last year's walks to recall precisely
this brown-dimpled swimming hole, let alone these
   twin power mowers

clenched together under a scruffy pine tree,
flecked with common rust stains—a pair of lovers
after a successful suicide pact? If
   I came more often

down to walk by the Andric, or else less often,
would I notice more of such alterations?
Something always changes, if only my own
   size, curve, and angle—

not that the boulder deigns to converse with me. Its
massive mossiness, welcoming and indifferent,
prompts me to stand stubbornly here, attempting
   to squeeze some blood out.

Blood? Blood from a stone? The pathetic fallacy
run amok? I know. But a modest history
does connect this boulder to my emotions.
   Late in the summer

of 1975, I hunched on its summit
(hunching, perching being the only options)
with a young man I introduced to anyone who would listen

as my editor. I recall he wore a
long dark cape which hindered his progress, surely,
as we clambered back down the rock. Oh, one thing
   led to another;

years passed, too, and now the black boulder seems if
not to meet my gaze or correct my memories
nonetheless to shift in its stony brook-bend
   ever so slightly.

Weathering

My mother had, I thought,
when I was growing up,
a uniform smooth surface like a rock
polished by waves. Or like
a flight of steps worn concave
at the center of each tread
she had been hollowed out.
This weathering, it took me years to see,
was neither luck nor personality.
Motherhood and years wear women down.
Either can alone;
but motherhood, although it saves no one,
mitigates the wear and tear somehow
with kindness—or with blindness. Take my hand
before we both are ground back into sand.

The Bruise

What happened to your arm?
asked in alarm.

Oh, my husband beats me black and blue.
Who knew?

An empty box I carried down the hall
bumped me. *Is that all?*

My easy bruising means I have anemia.
Not leukemia?

Domestic violence, cancer—
sensational, but not, alas, the answer.

These yellowing violet letters advertise
to the world's eyes

a fraction of my private history
mottled as mystery.

Broken blood vessels beneath the skin
signal "Come in.

Enter my flesh. Trace from each surface clue
inked in blotchy blue

inward to the minotaurish part,
my hidden heart."

I.D. Photo

Since I can feel my radiant nature shine
Out of my face as unmistakably
As sunlight, it comes as a shock to see
The features that apparently are mine.

Mirrors are not a lot of fun to pass,
And snapshots are much worse. Take the I.D.
Picture taken only yesterday
(Take it—I don't want it): sallow face

Pear-shaped from smiling—lumpy anyway,
Droopy, squinty. General discouragement.
I'd blame the painter, if this were in paint,
But can't avoid acknowledging it's me,

No likeness by an artist I could blame
For being bad at matching in with out.
What I see, alas, is what I get.
Victim and culprit are myself and time—

Having seen which, it's time to turn aside;
Look out from, not in at, an aging face
That happens to be mine. No more disgrace
Lies in having lived than having died.

Blemish

Beauty, discreet, keeps her proverbial secrets,
whereas an imperfection—seam, scab, scar—
broadcasts information
willy-nilly published on our skin.

Shamed by the revelation,
we have this consolation:
the world's reaction
is one more revelation.

When a cancer was burnt off
between my nose and mouth,
several men made a jovial suggestion:
"Did you cut yourself shaving?"

On the other hand,
"What happened to you?
Did you have a fall? Did someone hurt you?"
was the response of some women I knew.

But mostly women took one rapid look,
then slid their gaze aside.
Do not think there was no commiseration
just because not one syllable was said.

The Gift

Women in their fifties
are the recipients of an equivocal gift.
Not yet conspicuous for being decrepit,
we're evidently more than old enough
to turn transparent. And this new cloaked state
enables us to hear astonishing
news from friends, acquaintances, and sometimes
strangers, all of whom do not so much
look at as through us; lean in, then gaze out
over our shoulders in search of something
unseen, unseeable.
Why am I telling you this?
I more and more am asked. Because I'm here,
and am invisible. At just the moment
life draws one concealing curtain, though,
another veil is being lifted. Youth's
haze disperses, and I see distinctly
through the one-way mirror of the years.

Gay Witty Banter

A nightgowned child creeps partway down the stairs
and intercepted moans indignantly
"Everyone's down there having a good time
except for me."

On long car trips a similar refrain
can be heard:
"I have no one to talk to. Everyone
is sleeping or else driving. I am *bored.*"

Gay witty banter in the dining room:
she's in her element at nine or ten.
But kids and even grownups go to bed
and dinners, summers, even childhoods end

eventually. Then a father's dead.
Spectator-like, her head aswivel,
a silent mother watches
her teenage daughters quibble.

Guess which one tries desperately to scribble
with squeaky chalk on quiet's stubborn slate,
which one won't shut up?
The elder sister, staring at her plate,

in due course grows to be an editor
who cuts and clarifies and puts in order.
The younger one, the fidgeter, the whiner
grows into—no, already is—a talker,

poet, teacher, mother
who sprays her son with questions.
His father's a composer
whose native idiom

is witty but not chatty.
It takes her years to learn
it's possible to wake up in the night
and turn the nightlight on

and take a book and let it do the talking,
or take a pen
and paper and so chat
away until if necessary dawn.

The Yawn

When my son was an infant and he yawned,
I found I recognized (and only then—
never before till I became a mother)
how urgently this universal reflex
split open strangers' tired
faces on subway, bus, or street.

And though I was no Florence Nightingale
(neither, from what I've read,
was Florence Nightingale), I felt the urge
to take these men and women
into my arms, sling them over my shoulder,
pat and burp them till they fell asleep.

The Mother Verb

A Greek verb, *kamarono*—"strut" or "preen"—
also intransitively means "show off,"
"admire," "take pride in"—a rich constellation
circling a maternal connotation.
Specifically, it's often used of mothers
watching their children and especially

watching their children eat—particularly
eat the food their mothers have prepared.
Most specifically, watch their male children.
Even if they don't eat, their mothers watch.
Watching, of course, is far too pale a word.
They devour the children with their eyes.

The Nosebleed

Waiting for a Bennington light to change, I
saw, last week, a girl lean against a woman,
both blond, standing outside a supermarket.
Mother, bent over,

asked some question (all this I saw; heard nothing).
Before the light turned, I had divined the problem.
When she lifted her face to her mother: Bingo.
It *was* a nosebleed.

"It's still bleeding a little," the daughter answered
as we drove away. And I know the mother
bent again to offer the child a second
kleenex and kiss her.

Green light, green hills, we're driving north, it's summer.
Law enacted fleetingly in a rear-view
mirror no less powerful for its local
interpretation:

Love as rocking cradle that two can rest in,
bodies nested, cupped in one curve of shelter;
question, answer; need met as it arises.
Trouble breeds comfort.

Home is the Sailor

I want to go home, moaned the child,
the point of the story being he was at home.
Who hasn't felt nostalgic for the future,
homesick for a place we've never been?
Home from the sea, this little sailor longed
to be precisely where he was. But though
the place might not have changed, he had. Whatever
age glimmers gold has to be past or future;
touch it, it recedes. *Too many trees.*
Where are the houses? I don't like those blue
mountains, complained our son the first summer
he arrived in the country as a verbal being
able to hold a landscape in his head
against another, better one and say so.
He was two. That stubborn ache—I know it;
know the longing either to escape
or be more fully present. Both at once?
Here you are. I miss you.

The Land of Waiting

With thanks to Janna Malumud
Smith, *A Potent Spell,* and Andrew
Birkin, *Lost Boys; James M. Barrie
and the Love Story That Gave Birth to
Peter Pan*

The hour grew late. Her fear intensified.
Her husband went to bed. Unable to sleep,
the woman found a flashlight,
pulled on a sweater, followed
the long, uneven path down through the dew-
soaked grass to the dock, and stood
in the darkness waving the small beacon
to guide her grown boy home.

Some mothers carry flashlights
down to deserted piers
and pacing back and forth
scan the black water till dawn.
Some, like my friends and me,
sit it out in apartments,
listening for a key.

Such instances are mild.
The cell phone's been invented.
Our sons are not at war.
Nor are we alone
in living close to terror
(capital and small T).
Still, waiting is our country,

fear is our mother tongue.

With the whole town mourning
their drowning in the river,
Tom Sawyer, Huck, and Joe
attended their own funeral—
exceptional denouement
even for a happy ending.
But Aunt Polly's reaction—
rage grappling with her joy—
is perfectly realistic,
is in the lingua franca
understood by all
the citizens of waiting.

On holiday in Scotland
with the orphaned boys,
James Barrie used to panic
when periodically
Michael disappeared,
who'd "probably wandered off
to fish somewhere else,"
recalled a younger brother,
"and of course he was always
perfectly all right,
and wondered what the fuss
was all about," the fuss
being Barrie's cry,
"a haunting banshee wail,
Mi-i-ichael-l-l!"
echoing through the hills.

A few years later, Michael
became one of the boys
who never would grow old.
Naturalized long since
in the land of waiting,
Barrie was fluent in
the language of the place,
speaking it like a native,
even adding phrases
("the lost boys" being one)
which found a lasting home
in his adopted tongue.

Daylight Saving

It's time to change the time.
I've set the clocks ahead—
all but one, antique,
haughty on a high shelf,
that doesn't really run
but keeps its time to itself,
though it emits if touched
a crotchety, cracked chime.
My wristwatch will be last
to dutifully spring
forward—and we're all set,
as they say in Vermont. But wait:
my son is heading out.
Be home by one, I say.
And he replies: Okay,
one by the old time.

I wait in the slow zone
while he floats through another.
Is he an hour late?
Am I an hour ahead?
Either way, old mother,
It's time to go to bed.
The sleepy-feeling pace
(I turn a page and yawn)
is an illusion:
everyone's time runs
out at a single rate.

Not early and not late,
my son's abruptly back.

The Bond

The tact, the decorum, the gradual distancing
of parents and growing children
in their delicate dance of disengagement

tugs, repels both sides. By twelve or so
I could see clearly that my mother
preferred her best friend's company to mine,

but I moved past this pothole on the long
road of adolescent self-absorption,
so that by the time my mother died

and this same friend of hers could not conceal
her grief, but even more, her disappointment
that I, the daughter, should be such a dog

in the manger of the living, while her dear
friend was nowhere to be found—I think
I understood. I even sympathized.

This double memory helps me now I see
my son turn to his friends first, not to me,
as for that matter I turn first to mine,

not that the bond between
mother and daughter, mother and son
fails to pull taut every now and then,

and twang, and hum.

The Verge

Since her stroke, your mother calls the state
of things a mess, and who would disagree?
But where to put the age of gold's a challenge.
An iron law decrees past must be best,
Then must trump Now.

How dull and gloomy should this rule prove always true.
Let's devise another way to go,
back from the edge and into a green valley
where falling waters endlessly renew
their way, their weight, and redirect their flow

rinsed of the golden glow
nostalgia tints its icons with. Pristine,
these waters now run clear.
But run to where?
Upon belief and death and afterlife

lacking valedictory words, I wave
to her. She stands amid the tug of currents
at the verge. Lonely? Yes. Final? No.
Yes. No. We can't help looking backwards, though
time's law says sternly *Flow*.

Tea?

My brother is ill. I go to help him die.
This is mostly wrong, beginning with that *my*
(brother's all right). He isn't mine. And I
cannot escort him wherever he has to go
(where is he going?). Nevertheless, I fly
west through winter to help him somehow.
To help him; help myself; to do, to be
sisters, students, grandchildren: a frieze,
linked figures offering shared memories.

One such—from the late Fifties it would be,
in a diner in St. Johnsbury:
somebody at the table asks for tea,
whereupon the waitress, mysteriously
confounded by this order, echoes *Tea?*
in a sort of honking yodel.

Tea:
the word with which my brother answers me
when I ask Are you thirsty, Do you want
a cup, etcetera. I know he won't;
we're here because he has just put away
food and drink in favor of pure play,
conversation, memory, laughter, thought.
Brimming with the beverage never brought,
a ghostly teacup sends a plume of steam
curling and fragrant into the sickroom.

The White Cat

When the cat died, I glimpsed her constantly
out of the corner of my eye. I might
 be sitting at my table late at night;
a soft white ghost would silently pad by.

Dead people are less fugitive. In crowds
or by myself, drifting along a street,
I may at any time abruptly meet
my mother, friends—who, having shed their shrouds

and put on life, stroll down the avenue
nonchalantly. But as I approach,
when they are almost close enough to touch
I realize this is no one that I know,

but strangers, blank or poker-faced. Why not?
Who would solicit someone else's grief,
regret, and loss? And yet while we're alive
our loved ones vainly flap against the shut

eyes of the lover. Habit's filmy veil
blurs and dilutes our vision, though we bat
its folds away with spirit, like the cat
last seen in ghost form chasing her white tail.

Brimful

Scandalous, this joy
persisting day by day.
Do not ask me why.
It has to do with grey
and yellow: leaves that shine
against wet pavement; rain
stabbing its tiny needles
through a streetlight's beam.
Late this afternoon,
a razor edge of sun
threw a stone detail
I'd passed a thousand times into relief.
It has to do with fullness:
everything I see,
brimming with itself,
overflows as radiance.
How else is it my mother,
my father, all my dead
are glowing now like lamps?
What from close up was smoke—
choking and panic, guttering and grief—
from here feels calm, benign,
haloed with the gleam
of what is fast becoming long ago,
of what, all suffering ended,
turns around to light the darkness up.

Return

In Barbara Pym's *Quartet in Autumn,* Marsha,
who likes to hoard some items (empty milk
bottles in her shed and filmy nightgowns

in a drawer), maintains a scrupulous balance
by surreptitiously returning others:
an empty catfood tin to a library shelf.

Give back. Go back in thought. Revert. Restore.
Return, return to the capital for the winter,
one's longed-for paradise at any season.

October 1949: George Orwell
writes of his plans to find a pied-a-terre
and so return to London for the winter:

Hebridean winters are too harsh.
But his London life is over.
He has three months to live.

May 1992: my mother talks
of going up to the country by mid-June.
But her return to Vermont is in an urn.

There is a season, turn, turn.
Oh earth, oh earth, return.
Took from his eyes the dawn of his return.

Lightbulbs and Soap

September: sunny afternoon.
Stroll with my sister once again.

Drained by two hours of angry sleep,
limp, drowsy, I less stroll than droop.

Watch out, though. Something fin-like slides
up from the river as if to slice

our futures. Hers is granite; mine
is thorns and mist. It cuts through both.

Are we bleeding? Neither one
would deign to blot the other's wound.

Fishing for any common theme
of talk—they're few and far between—

we come up with the legacy
our mother left to her and me.

Lightbulbs and soap was her advice
to her: bring these to any place

you move to. Mine is little more:
she taught me what white lies are.

Precepts still valid, sturdy, sound,
but pretty meager on the ground.

In a nest of teachers, writers,
what has happened to the talkers?

Lightbulbs and soap: a terse still life
rendered in tight-lipped black and white.

Lightbulbs in a fruitbowl; lies
like white lilac in a vase

with maybe a single stoic bar
of soap; a tablecloth; no more.

Our livelihood, our medium—where
has language gone? Into thin air

floated away, and left a frail
dusting of tiny crumbs—faint trail

for our twin tracking through the wood
our mother with her heavy tread

and upright carriage paced into
and vanished ahead of us two.

Gone with her words into the dark?
We're squinting in the sunny park.

Meanwhile a mile or two uptown:
a primal scene, our very own.

Two sisters shared a dark ground-floor
bedroom they left by the same door,

emerging into different lives
and separate sets of memories,

even of what our mother said
before she joined the silent dead.

The Ice Princess

My inner bitch, as cold as ice,
is always the most pitiless
when she contemplates the ends
of lives of parents of her friends.

It was his time to go, she'll say.
Or *Why prolong her agony?*
As if the genre elegy
had never meant a thing to me;

as if I'd never wished, with tears,
to have had my father a few more years;
as if my mother's stoical
silence had been the best of all

endings. I tell her: *Let them go*
with no more censorship from you.
It's true I hope, when death draws close,
to exit with as little fuss,

as promptly as my parents did.
Tardy or prompt, we end up dead,
I remind my ice princess,
and reprimand her ruthlessness.

III

The Worry Box

A New York kindergartner,
fearful since the attacks,
is told "Just write your worry down
and put it in this box"

("it" being the folded paper,
being, also, her fear),
the designated Worry Box
her mother bought for her.

I first encountered it, I think,
in a book on meditation,
this notion of consigning
negative information

to words scrawled on a sheet of paper
which you then insert
into some neutral vessel—whence
it loses the power to hurt.

A radical variation
on the Worry Box idea
says take the paper, burn it, scatter
its ashes in the air:

poof! goes your trouble. An unsent
letter can cause no danger.
This version of the Worry Box
appealed to the forest ranger,

except the page she set on fire
she prematurely let
float out into the bone-dry scrub
while it was still alight.

What was this problem paper?
She claimed it was a letter
from her ex-husband; whatever it said,
she burned it to feel better.

But this is only Version Two
of what the ranger said.
In Version Three she lit a match
and watched the fire spread

not over one small letter
but acres which became
(winds shifting in the crisp-parched hills)
a swirling wall of flame.

But this is only Version Three.
In Version One, she'd smelled
smoke which she traced to a campfire
still smoldering in a field.

These versions' variables
are innocence or blame;
they all seemed touched by passion,
or torched, if we mix flame

and roiling smoke with inner heat.
Anger, grief, desire:
sap boils, cause bubbles with effect.
Where there's smoke there's fire.

Newspaper photos give no clue
to what might lie beneath
her round face, sweet expression,
blond hair, clear skin, good teeth.

Was she a virgin tablet
on which old wrongs were scored
(and whose wrongs?) or a victim?
What was the magic word

secreted in her private stash?
We all, since that September,
have inner hideouts where we cram
both what we must remember

and what we wish would disappear,
would vanish in thin air
(ominous word): just vaporize.
The precious mingles there

with the unspeakable; cherishing
mindmelds with, morphs to terror.
What did the kindergartner—
before she handed over

her sheet of construction paper—
record so trustingly?
Her mother, who longed to take a peek
(who wouldn't?), stealthily

opened her daughter's Worry Box
and stole a hurried look.
Surprise: she saw sharp orange flames
and billowing black smoke.

Or: two tall buildings both on fire.
Or: one short printed word,
four letters long, in capitals,
black on an orange field.

Life goes on. Anxious, hopeful,
the loving mother locks
the paper up and goes to work,
with her own Worry Box,

invisible but weighty,
ubiquitous as the cell
phones the whole world carries now,
waiting for what dread call?

Born with the scribe's remorseless urge
to search and find the right
words, get the experience down
somehow in black and white,

should I feel vindicated
when we're told to represent
our greatest fear, then lock it up
either as punishment

or apotropaic magic—
or are the two the same?
The page is smoking. Careful!
Will the box burst into flame

which may then spread beyond control?
Whole mountainsides, we learn,
are not immune. Entire states
apparently can burn,

so why not a whole country?
One woman's private pain
leapfrogs from tree to forest
like fire through gasoline

or like the towers collapsing
in an avalanche of heat
bursting from what locked vessel
white-hot with rage and hate?

Hayman, Show Low, Durango,
the fiery necklace grows.
A restless wind is blowing.
Who can control the blaze?

A New York kindergartner,
fearful since the attacks,
is told to write her worries down
and put them in a box.

Impatience

Late in the month, late afternoon,
en route or waiting for the train,
spring barely peeking through mild rain:
what does this impatience mean?

Scarlet eruptions on the skin.
We're poised: when will the war begin?
I crane to hear the starting gun.
What does this impatience mean?

Wait for the other shoe to drop.
What now is green will soon be ripe;
what's ripening began as green,
so what does this impatience mean?

Is the best potion for the hurt
of life in time to stay alert
or try to sleep to ease the strain,
the rash, the spring, the war, the rain,

oh what does this impatience mean?

Travellers

As a dog turns three times before sleep,
restless, uneasy, easily distracted,
I look around: who'll be my fellow voyagers
in what might just as well be Charon's boat?

Think of the rites performed as we depart.
Take off your shoes. Pad through an empty door-
frame. And—a specially Stygian detail—
coins in your pocket? Scoop. Deposit here.

A man sits weeping in a plastic chair
in—is this a departure lounge? a gate?
Names in this chilly chamber don't adhere
to what they label. Hours go by. En route,

I spy a neighbor knitting something long
and purple (mad Ophelia!) and hear
the needles click—or would, but for the roar
of Charon's winged rowboat in midair.

River's Edge

One of the faithful who listen
to the lapping of the Hudson
in October when the sun slants low,
I stretched out on a little cement jetty
not much wider or longer than my body
and fell asleep in the squint and sparkle
and dreamed. Staircases; doorways;
wrought-iron railings. Every now and then
a tall intruder in a yellow jacket
interposed between the sun and me.
Why are we drawn to edges?
I opened my eyes. It was still afternoon.
Low in the water, a black barge was passing,

Boatride

Here's a new book about Catullus.
Among the things the index tells us:

the light that shone from one old book
is guttering and going out

(dim meta-criticism—not
the blazing words the poet wrote).

Where's *Poets in a Landscape?* Lost.
Or *Uses of Enchantment*—tossed

overboard to ease the load
of what we ask the young to read?

For, starting with the fairy tale,
a course in Children's Lit last fall

strongly suggested Bettelheim
was drifting swiftly down the same

stream—soon, with Highet, to join the crew
of ghostly passengers paddled through

Lethe's thronged postmodern dark
in Professor Charon's bark,

learned shades murmuring as they float
willy-nilly in that black boat,

steep banks on either side. One sees
bare ruined choirs of indices,

each thorny thicket (forest? tree?)
entangling some anthology.

History's out, the present's in,
or "presentism" (the new term).

The travellers no longer need
neologisms, being dead,

voyaging on the dim endless
river of forgetfulness.

Dr. Mnemosyne's Office

Patience and Fortitude,
two dogs, one black, one golden,
pace from room to room,
Prometheus, Epimethus,
names designed to be
forgotten. One by one
they put their heads in your lap,
gaze at you soulfully.
Then one of the two turns,
Time and Eternity,
and pads away into the inner room
whose air prognoses darken
and with a sign lies down
under Dr. Memory's glossy desk
which without warning morphs into a boat,
a lonely ghost boat paddling upstream
through morning mist, though it is afternoon,
over the river of oblivion.

Triolets In the Argolid

Return

The taste is strong as ever,
figs and cheese and wine.
I recall each savor;
the taste is strong as ever,
even if it will never
be quite so fresh again.
The taste is strong as ever,
figs and cheese and wine.

Obverse

Two sides of one coin
love and worry seem.
Both of them are mine:
two sides of one coin,
two links in one chain,
left/right of one brain?
Two sides of one coin
love and worry seem.

Metamorphosis

Why does transformation
sneak up on us so?
In life, not just narration,

why does transformation
creep up—yes, in slow motion,
inexorably, though?
Why does transformation
sneak up on us so?

Technology

Where are worry beads
now people have cell phones
clamped against their heads?
Where are worry beads?
Ancient human needs,
new millennium;
where are worry beads?
People have cell phones.

Fortress

Before we reach the top,
street sounds fade away.
Many steep steps up
before we reach the top;
just when did they stop?
Silence; scalding sky.
Before we reach the top,
street sounds fade away.

Dactylic

Tino's counting on his fingers.
Syllables and rhyme;
a faint Sapphic cadence lingers.
Tino's counting on his fingers.
Generations of singers
keeping, conquering time.
Tino's counting on his fingers;
syllables and rhyme.

And All the Ways Grew Dark

Sunset. We ride the bus
through the Argolid
skirting an abyss.
Sunset: we ride the bus,
pondering, each of us,
thoughts written down, not said.
Sunset: we ride the bus
through the Argolid.

The Shadow of Departure

The same old hole in the shape
of a father punched into his heart,
his hungry eye raking to fill the void,
Telemachus stood up and faced the crowd.

After he sailed away, his old nurse kept
the news from Penelope as long as she could
(it wasn't long), who thereupon
climbed to her bedroom through the gulf of pain

his absence had unlocked, and wailed, and napped,
and woke and wept, slept, dreamed, and woke again.
Thetis quick as thought
shot up from the depths of the cold silver sea

to ease her boy's intractable heartache,
did what she could (it wasn't much), and stole
and kept on stealing glances at his face.
Tightened to its extreme, what would it mean,

the knot between a mother and a son?
Pleasure pierced with grief—
no space between them but a grudging sliver
too close for him, not close enough for her.

To chat or nod or smile—all are a strain;
to look at you beside me on the bench
(and side by side means glances slip and slide)
as we sit in the station waiting for the train.

Boy Heroes in the Sea

With thanks to Simonides and Wallace Stevens as
well as Elian Gonzalez and the relatives

... when in the wrought chest
the wind blowing over
and the sea heaving
struck with her fear, her cheeks not dry,
she put her arm over him and spoke:
My child, such trouble I have.

Icon of wishes, angel face, oh gold
beyond the currency of flesh and blood
invested with desire
for what is the dispute;

tender of memory all
the dreamers of the island longed to hold,
clasp, keep beyond the tidal lap of change;

If it was only the outer voice of the sky
and cloud ... but it was more than that,
more even than her voice.

And you sleep, your heart is placid,
you dream in the joyless wood;
in the night nailed in bronze,
in the dark blue you lie still and shine.

History's storm and counterblast,

emblems, banners, rumors, semaphores,
incident, episode, lesson, operetta
stiffened to purgatorial parade,
each actor labeled, carrying a sign,
while innocence is pouting out of reach—
protection! time is limited.

If this
danger were a danger to you,
your small ear would attend my words.
But I tell you: sleep, my baby, and let
our trouble sleep.

   And also:
tell me, if you know,
Why, when the singing ended and we turned
Toward the town, tell why the glassy lights,
The lights in the fishing boats at anchor there . . .
Mastered the night and portioned out the sea,
Fixing emblazoned zones and fiery poles. . .

Dolphins and dreams. The legend of the lost
and found. The given image of salvation
washed up and caught and cherished.
How to let go of what was freely given?
Yet the embrace, the deadlock must be broken.
Let some change, said Danae, *appear,*
Zeus father, from you. And so it did:
the hero iconized at first as infant
grown up as a savior, sandalled, helmeted,
slayer of monsters, rescuer of maidens,
this change imbuing the sea's changeable

enchanting brew of story, her deep voice,
wave-colored, cresting, blowing off in foam,
Arranging, deepening, enchanting night.

Three Roads

And on your right the place where three roads met.
Look down—the valley, there.
We passengers to Delphi crane our necks.
No one can say precisely where.

As well as roadside shrines and blossoming trees,
the highway winding round the mountain is
dotted with decisions and transitions,
some totally invisible, some less.

Look hard enough: it's possible to see
more than the season shifting stealthily.
Back home my brother slowly, slowly walks
toward the subterranean river; takes

an oar . . . the oracle? We'll be there soon.
No one can predict precisely when.
Silence seals each mortal afternoon.

Embarkation

Conversation with my brother
as he prepares to cross the river:

"Which poems did you teach today?
Hardy? Frost? Read some to me."

I read to him. We say Goodbye,
I love you. Do I hear a sigh?

A breath expelled—not word, not moan—
then Debbie takes the telephone

(there's always someone by the bed)
and family picks up the thread,

making our several ways through winter
to keep him company to the water.

The rowboat is too small for more
than one; and Zeno on the shore

stands with a stopwatch: A to Z?
First try to get from A to B.

Clearly, the goal is out of reach.
Yet David does attain the beach.

He lets go of each helping hand
and steps across the sucking sand

into the boat, and waves to us,
and smiles; then turns and vanishes.

Conklin 455, 3:55 PM, Wednesday, March 3, 2004

Hardy's kneeling oxen; Merrill's sword
dangling death over the youth in bed;
Frost's lover hankering for a counter-word;
Ransom's white geese that cried in goose Alas—

you poems we read my brother in those last
phone calls, so that instead of silences
the valedictory music of each phrase
filled his weeks and days,

help me today, please. Come with me to class.
Up two flights to Conklin Hall, fourth floor.
Pause; door is closed. Regroup. It's five to four.
Remember who is waiting for me there.

David, who died twelve hours ago,
is part of me, and I am part of you,
Serene, Muhammad, Gladies, Osner, Chad.
I offer you no more than what I've had

lavished on me. Love what you give away:
aha! you get to keep it till you die.
The keeping is synonymous with giving.
My brother gave as long as he was living,

and longer, after, more.
I open the door.

Horace I.24

A dear friend gone: does grief require restraint?
Oh Muse of mourning, teach us a complaint,
Make music of our loss,
Sing in your clear sweet voice.

And so Quintilius sleeps perpetually.
When will integrity and loyalty
(Sister to justice), dignity, decorum
Find anyone to equal him?

His death was the occasion of a flood
Of tears. But he was never ours for good,
Virgil, so you weep and sob in vain;
He can't come back again.

Even were you to play with greater grace
Than Orpheus, whose lyre enchanted trees,
No life blood would flow back
Into the empty shade, once the grim crook

Of the soul-shepherd god had forced it in
To huddle with the rest in his dark pen.
Yes, it is hard. But patiently
Is the best way of bearing what must be.

Black Dream

Italicized portions are from Sappho
Fragment 26, translated by Diane Rayor

Black Dream, you come...and when sleep...
A dream's a printout of a memory,
A memory an icon of a dream.

Sweet god, wonderfully from sorrow... Last week
My brother returned from the dead in a green car.
It was late June: a close and starless night

And also afternoon. He pulled up the damp driveway
And I helped him out and carried him into the house
No bigger in my arms than a cat or a baby

But also large as life.
As is well known, such visits are fleeting.
The dead can't stay till dawn.

Did he climb back into the car and drive away?
To keep separate the power...
He was and was not an independent body.

Black Dream, you come ... the car was green as hope,
Green as a remembered lawn at Bread Loaf
Behind the theater. A little pool

Had been scooped out of the turf and lined with stones;
A miniature fountain gurgled in the middle.
It all was ceremonial but tiny.

Posed, apparently, behind this pool
In a snapshot from 1957 or so,
My parents stand side by side with grave expressions.

Her brown braids are wound around her head.
He has his seersucker summer jacket on
And his white buck shoes.

Who posed them, snapped the picture?
My older sister? Could it have been me?
Black Dream . . . the pair stand solemnly as if

About to undergo some ceremony
Connected with the pool, although the pool
Is small enough for them to have stepped right over

Had they not been immobilized by sleep or death.
It is about the same size as the pools
In the Wood Between the Worlds

In *The Magician's Nephew*.
Some of those pools are only ankle deep,
Nor is the water wet. But if you jump

Into the right pool touching the right magic
In order to keep separate the power
You're utterly transported:

Down, down you go (the pool now has no bottom)
And then emerge into the light of an unfamiliar sun
In a world which may be newer or older than ours but is other.

Wet green lawn; quiet place where nothing happens.
Driveway to the summer house where dreams
Flourish like mushrooms in the damp of sleep;

My parents risen from the pool, my brother
Driving up the slope, the black and white
Of icon and the little car grass green.

My husband, waking from a recent nap,
Exclaims that for the first time ever, he
Has dreamed in living color: gold and green.

Hope's Last Words

October afternoon—I'm walking—green,
dappled light in early afternoon.
My old friend's mother, Hope,
soft and sharp and peach-fuzz faced; not sweet;
motherly, weaponly, whose round blue eyes,
embracing and enquiring and accusing,
seemed to miss nothing, died this week. Her final
words, her daughter told me (Hope was running
out of breath, but could begin a sentence
surely not intended as her last,
although who knows such things?), were: *I was thinking. . .*
That ended it: the phrase but not the thought.
The thought was just beginning. Did she sense
that death was fluttering lightly near her lips,
and did she therefore shape those syllables
with more attention as they floated out
to greet the listener? And another question:
how is it that when our beloved dead
are no longer within reach or earshot,
their sentences left permanently unfinished,
how can we bear the change? How can we shoulder
the emptiness and still go marching forward?
Hope at a hundred knew or thought she knew
something. She isn't telling, though; not now,
not yet, no longer. Honey of October
green and gold, and darkness coming on.

Hummingbird

With thanks to *Greek Lyrics*, translated by
Richmond Lattimore, and *Hummingbirds in the
Garden,* by Roma Gans

The hummingbird, *archilochus colubris,*
a buzz of brevity, loop arrow zoom,
glints and is gone, the blotch of shimmering scarlet
as if from too long staring at the sun;
the stab of sweetness and the standing still
in air, a *route of evanescence.* Who
could help aping Emily Dickinson on this subject?
Other poets flock to mind as well.
Appropriately, the Ruby-throat's scientific
namesake, Archilochus, was a lyric poet.
Zesty, rebarbative, he sang of war,
poverty, passion, vengeance. Whereas
the buzzing busyness of the hummingbird,
its radiant witchery, rather call to mind
Sappho's Aphrodite's golden chariot
yoked to sparrows, *who fairly drew* the goddess
down in speed aslant the black world, the bright air
trembling at the heart to the pulse of countless
fluttering wingbeats. Were those really sparrows?
Did Sappho know of hummingbirds? If so,
maybe it was she with a glint of wit
who named the species after her rough and ready
colleague from Paros.

Another lyric poet,
Theognis of Megara, conceived of birdflight
not in terms of love but fame, although
fame bestowed for the sake of love. So long as
you take care, like Lattimore, to translate
a crucial verb as "hover"
rather than "float" or "fly," it isn't hard
to find the hummingbird in Theognis' poems
not now drawing a chariot
or flitting from flower to flower,
but touring the wide world, air, islands, ocean:
See, I have given you wings on which to hover uplifted
high above earth entire and the great waste of the sea
without strain, whereupon the gift of flight
swiftly morphs into melody.

Fame; beauty; song—all roughly apposites.
Wherever men meet in festivals, as men
gather, you will be there, your name will be spoken again
as the young singers, with the flutes clear piping beside them,
make you into a part of the winsome verses . . .
Flight as song; song as flight. The hummingbird
doesn't sing; its beating wings are its voice.
It doesn't walk. *It uses its feet*
only to hold onto a twig when it rests.
It can only feed when flying,
and it flies all day long,
steering toward sustenance: the color red
or nectar, with those wings that beat
Sixty times in one second, so fast you can see only a blur.
A hummingbird can tilt its wings.
It can tilt them up and back.

It can flip them over so the underside
points toward the sky.
That turning, so the earth side faces heaven;
the detail that *small insects caught in the sticky nectar* . . .
are the meat in the meals of hummingbirds . . .

Why am I making such heavy weather
of the obvious? *Nektar:*
deathless. *Ambrosia:* immortal.
Food of the gods. An epic pantheon
compressed to frantic lyric brevity—
no wonder it buzzes like a bee caught in a jar.

Euripides' choruses often yearn
to fly away like birds
in order to escape the ills of mortals.
The birds of Aristophanes have escaped.
The hummingbird flickers between earth and heaven,
an urgent visitor, ruthless, fugitive,
heated, hungry: blushing and then gone.

The Street of the Muses

for Jason Stallings Psaropoulos

The Muses know your mother well.
As their beloved acolyte,
She has a good eye for the mess
That happens when they're not

Fully in charge. "The Anti-Muses
Are out in force," she likes to say
When passports fly into black holes
And best-laid plans all go astray.

Lately, dear child, it's evident
The Anti-Muses have agreed
To color-code disorder to
A deeper shade of dread:

Daily bomb threats, vile videos . . .
Yet the true Muses, though discreet,
Ply their good magic. Under their
Protection, on their very street,

In a sealed box of innocence
Like infant Perseus afloat
In the carved chest, you feed and grow
And sleep: you incubate.

Bedding down in a sacred spot—
An ancient form of divination:
Sleep and the god will send a dream—
Used to be known as incubation.

In ancient Athens, spanking new,
How much has changed? From your long dream
You'll wake to faces, voices, names
The day you journey home—

Triumphant trip, and inspiration
(The Muses smile) for many a new
Victory ode of hope and joy
For, little Jason, you.

Strangely, all this will fade away.
The Muses' mother, Memory,
Must quickly clear your busy brain
To hold our crowded century.

But first, showered with the Muses' gifts,
Feast! Multitask, or pick and choose—
All arts surround you. From their street
You've moved into the Muses' house.

Raised in that haven, lucky boy,
You'll face the labyrinth of harm
And bliss—our birthright—not alone
But with the Muses' powerful charm.

Neolithic Figurine, Spetses Archaeological Museum

Winged, bronze, two inches tall or less;
embodied stillness brimming with repose;
you have no feet, but at your pedestal
lie a row of slim bronze objects all
like you unlabelled: skewer, spoon, and snake,
what looks to be a zipper pull; fishhook—
each clearly fashioned by a human hand
for some earthly purpose. But you stand
perpendicularly poised for flight,
arms ready to reach out and wings to beat.

Pawn-sized messenger and angel too,
your energy compressed inside of you
for two millennia, with what look to be
both tenderness and generosity
(the tiny tilted head, the earnest gaze)—
I trust you, though you haven't any face.
Though you could fit into a toddler's hand,
I write in the belief you understand,
and greet you, goddess, there in your glass case
upstairs in a Spetsiot captain's house.
Where were you on this island before that?
Before, before . . . how many summers' heat?
June, July, August: centuries go by.
From your corner can you see the sky?

Modern Greek 101

These phrases, once lodged in your memory,
Will help you find your way, I guarantee,
Through any social circumstance in Greek,
Each Scylla and Charybdis when you speak.
All will work in any situation,
Plug up gaps in any conversation,
Politely answer any salutation.
It's surely no coincidence all four
In different ways purport to reassure.
So get your notebooks out, for here they are.

Siga-siga first: take it easy, slow
Down. *Ti na kanome:* what can we do?
Then *pirazi:* it doesn't matter.
(See how our repertory's getting fatter?)
Last but not least *en daxi:* all right, okay.
These are the crucial ones, and this is why:
Whichever of the four you chance to use
Shrugs with a weary grace you can't refuse,
An attitude for which there is no name
In English, though we try it all the same,
Not understanding what we imitate:
Mild acquiescence in the face of Fate,
Not dialectical and not dramatic,
But unassuming, formulaic, phatic.

One boiling morning I remarked, "It's hot."
The aproned landlord shrugged: "It matters not."

"What a pretty evening," I once said.
"What can we do?" a black-clad crone replied.
Reverse these scraps of dialogue: you too
Can answer anything that's said to you—
Though *said* is not the word so much as *sung:*
A whole philosophy rolls off the tongue.

Rachel Hadas studied classics at Harvard, poetry at Johns Hopkins, and comparative literature at Princeton. Between college and graduate school she spent four years in Greece, an experience that surfaces variously in much of her work. Since 1981 she has taught in the English Department of the Newark (NJ) campus of Rutgers University, and has also taught occasional courses in both literature and writing at Columbia and Princeton, as well as sometimes serving on the poetry faculty of the Sewanee Writers' Conference. The author of twelve books of poetry, essays, and translations, she is the recipient of honors including a Guggenheim Fellowship in Poetry, an Ingram Merrill Foundation grant in poetry, and an award in literature from the American Academy and Institute of Arts and Letters. Her collections of poetry include *Laws* (Zoo Press, 2004); *Indelible* (2001); *Halfway Down the Hall: New & Selected Poems* (1998), which was a finalist for the 1999 Lenore Marshall Poetry Prize; *The Empty Bed* (1995); *The Double Legacy* (1995); *Mirrors of Astonishment* (1992); and *Living in Time* (1990).